Under the Sugarloaf

Rosy Wilson

CB

First published in 2006
Copyright @ Rosy Wilson (poems) 2006 and
@ Paul Haydock-Wilson (etchings) 2006

C. Boland
2, Churchview
Wicklow Town
Co. Wicklow

A CIP catalogue record for this book
is available from the British Library

ISBN 0-9543878-7-2

Cover painting by Paul Haydock-Wilson
Cover design by Carol Boland

Printed and bound in Ireland by
Ruon Print Ltd

For all my family and friends

Acknowledgement is given to the following
publications where some of these poems, or versions
of them have appeared:
*The Stinging Fly, Writing Women, Jumping the Bus
Queue, Wildside, Dulwich and Ripley Poetry
anthologies, Leaf Poems, Voyages, Rising Tide,
High Tide, Away from the Tribe.*

Rosy Wilson lives in the shadow of the Sugarloaf in County Wicklow. She is a director and a volunteer at Glencree Centre for Peace and Reconciliation, and a long term member of Amnesty International.
In 2000, Rosy was one of Poetry Ireland's Introduction Poets. **Under the Sugarloaf** is her first collection.

Paul Haydock-Wilson is an artist and printmaker, working in London and County Wicklow. He exhibits in Kilmantin Arts in Wicklow Town, and in London galleries. In 2006, Paul exhibited his etchings in the Royal Academy's Summer Exhibition.

For their help and encouragement,
I wish to thank the Shed Poets.
Mimi Khalvati, Paula Meehan and
Catherine Phil MacCarthy.

Contents

Play On

Etchings in response to poems

This evening's gift

This evening's gift

In the dark, as I drive
from Glencree thinking
of reconciliation for
Tel Aviv, Ramallah,

of peace in Darfur,
I'm not ready for a curve
in the road, stir in a hedge,
stare of a young deer,

velvet fur grey
in crescent moon light
muzzle and soft lips raised
aware but not afraid.

I draw up more
surprised than the deer,
he hoofs across the road
graceful as a dancer

turns, waits on the edge,
another steps out,
a sister or brother,
and follows the first.

I bring this picture home -
the valley's present.

Swans in Bray Harbour

Swans are resting in Bray Harbour
as if they've settled all those messages
wayward deities used send them on.
They're weary of the symbolism

of poetry, don't even want to swim
in couples to support the claim
monogamy is right for birds and women.
This bunch of ragged swans are lame

ducks compared with Yeats' nine and fifty
wild ones counted on a Coole Park Lake.
They're not wheeling in great broken rings
they've fallen from grace, lack ambition,

beaks pecking wings, necks curved down
not mysterious, beautiful, in no way living up
to their image, making you wonder
with their off-white feathers,

washed-out wings, how gods and artists
ever chose this species that lacks
a skylark's flight, a thrush's song, colours
of robins, blue tits or goldfinches.

I shift my seat on rocks above the harbour
stretch veined legs, brush sea-dust from trousers
call to the birds in praise of ruffling feathers
unstringing nets of legend, pulling together.

Assumption

It's Lady Day
and lazily, on holiday,
I lie beside the cairn

watch little blues fly
swallows play,
feel gorse shoots
with golden buds

pick up between
the twisted charcoal roots
remnants of last summer's
mountain fires.

Now heathers flower again
white and mauve as evening
sunlight over Dublin Bay.
I breathe in mountain air

and scan the Sugarloaf
for outlines of our kids
zig-zagging up

then follow sheep paths on,
skirting the brow
of Carraigoona.

Cirque du Soleil

I watch them jump, spin,
somersault across the stage;
a trapeze artist swings over,
lifts a girl through a trapdoor,
holds her high like a prize.

Dancers in white robes circle,
escort her through red curtains,
she sings an old chanson,
Je ne regret rien,
her theme song.

I imagine tiptoeing
round the trap close to its edge,
sense immersion - suck, squelch
black mud, quagmire, remember
another time when trespassing

in De Valera's garden,
I fell into his duck pond
up to my neck in smelly water.
The bottomless ooze closed in
and I heard my brother's words,

'She's a goner.' His friend
pulled me out, held me up.
Every night Dev's lights shone
through my bedroom window
searching.

Meeting at Wavelengths

Is *that gin? We have one*
before going out
another when we come home
after our swim.

I sip from my plastic bottle
raspberry flavoured still water.
Yes it's gin, helps me stay afloat
have my whiskey after work at night.

Well you would, you're still young
fine figure you have, wish I was
young with you. I know how to treat
most men who eye me like that

but laugh with my eighty year old
admirer and his stooped wife
hope I'll still swim in these baths
at their time of life

then see as I change
sagging breasts
belly spread into middle age
brambles of veins twining my legs

from pubes to instep, clusters
of blackberries behind the calves
and hang up my costume
red as geraniums.

She is young and beautiful

All day, back bent over tub,
she scrubs, drubs clothes,
rubs them on a wooden board
wringing their linen in her
hard-worked hands.

She pauses to rest a minute,
stretches muscled arms,
heaves a sigh, up to her elbows
in thankless washing.

She welcomes the visit
of her sister-maid coming
downstairs shouldering
another bundle of laundry.

On this busy day there's no
spare time to talk, unlike those
mondays when they rubbed clothes

with stones in the running stream
together in open air, gossiping,
singing wash songs.

After *The Wash House* by William Orpen
National Gallery of Ireland

Connemara Trout

Fish glide and glisten
        one has made the leap
rests on rougher rock

        moss green,
                jade green,
                        leaf green,

looking down on liquid stone.

Two others struggle
                        through tunnels
upwater,
        against the tide.

This off-cut of an altar table
                                is sacred
as fish etched on stone
                        of celtic cross
                                or catacomb,
sacred as this green land
                        marbled
with veins of earth.

Sculpture by Albert Power

Shade

It's a walk with a friend on the muddy path
beside a river, a rough drawn border,
between her field with the Hereford herd
and my kitchen garden dug over.

It's the sight of a hare leaping through grass,
of a sparrow pecking birdseed off stone
or resting in saxifrage, undisturbed.
It's the fur of a bulldog chewing a bone.

It's the colour of work in a timber study,
of bookshelves stocked in no given order,
mahogany desk in a shaded corner
where leaves shake outside on winter alder.

It's the shade of hair in my photo of Father
who died too young and left us together.

Hygieia the Healer

I wake up early, push
through bracken and whin
take the rocky track to the cairn
a red ball rises from the sea
stripes the horizon.

       I dive into bright waters
       let tides pull me down
       to an underworld cave
       fish swim through my fingers
       I float in a dolphin's shade.

The goddess waits on the shore
gives me her remedy of
mistletoe or oak sperm.

Good Friday Agreement

Snow falls beyond the hour
       late daffodils behind barbed wire.

Red hand on leaders' shoulders
       pushing hard around the borders.

Stations of the Cross, Father forgive them
       ravelling a process – prisoners, victims.

Women are keening, garnering their
       children's bodies for public burial,

gathering as the tomb empties,
       intercepting gardeners in cemeteries.

Party leaders have agreed to weave
       three strands - they wave and leave.

At Easter Masses heads are raised,
       the closing stone is rolled away.

At Easter time the sun was said
       to dance a jig on the rim of the world.

You have to be in love to write poetry *

You ask me my source
and I answer it's love
that makes the river run,
water fall, fountains flow over.

Love drops rain on purple roses,
on poppies' paper blouses,
sprinkles dew on the lawn,
tears on white pages.

When the source runs dry
my land becomes caked mud,
barely a trickle in the cracks.
I can't find the words.

You show me a Chinese landscape
of mudflats under the moon
where a lotus flower blooms
alone.

*Raymond Carver

Last Evening

you walked onto the sunset beach
I watched as a pale mist

sprinkled down and you became
a shadow fading into grey sea

you are no longer here
even in my memory

I cannot sculpt the cheekbones
I stroked a thousand ways

or paint your lips I used to kiss
every night and day

or mould your body that lay with mine
all our years together.

Today I follow your steps
in the drifting sand

which holds no footprints
my cracked-skin fingers

dig and sift
build castles in the air

strand my grey hair
with strips of seaweed.

Grey Stones

The sun was shining earlier this morning
but now rain's falling on my book and pen
words are splotched
damp pages will not hold blue ink.

I sing the blues to bridge our absences
but these are drowned in rhythms of
grey waves sounding, resounding
on the pebbled beach

and listen to the waves
the to and fro' of them, their undertow
drawing over banks of shifting stones.

How often have we walked together here
my head in air, breathing in the sea
yours bent to study stones around your feet.

You pick up quartz, flint, quartzite,
every now and then you find a jewel,
hold an agate up against the light,
put it in your pocket with the rest.

I strip, put on a red costume,
run down shelves until my navel's wet
then dive under; waves rock me
as I breaststroke further in.

Will you be there to hold my towel,
rub cold shoulders,
wrap goose-pimpled arms
when I crawl out.

Love Poem

This morning,
love
was like eating
ripe avocado pears,
dressed
and seasoned
with olive oil,
lemon juice,
basil and
black pepper,
spooning towards
the centre
where the seed has been.

Raking

The back lawn, since my absence, is a field
so I work to cut it down to size but
as I try to pull out trails of bindweed,
and dig up couch that's smothering the roses

an autumn leaf, a trefoil, gently glazed,
jumps just in front of my rake's steel tines,
I stop and gaze - the frog stays very still,
brown burnets flutter over singing wrens.

After all those years of work in London
this place has wrapped itself around my shoulders
as I look up towards the Wicklow hills
or count ships sailing out beyond Bray Harbour,

contented to be over on my own,
although aware that it's from you I learned
close observation of all natural objects -
I watch the frog and wait for your return.

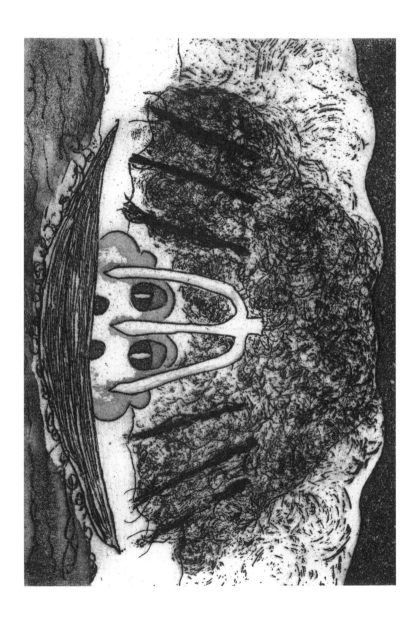

Leaning into Evening

Leaning into evening I switch on the News
in time for the Angelus,

a minute's break as people pause
from cooking dinners, waiting for bread to rise

or driving a tractor home. I remember schooldays,
all of us reciting out loud, *The Angel of the Lord . . .*

but that was long ago, now I forget the end
though I'll stay still, say a short prayer

for children, their children. Leaning into evening
I draw curtains, turn on lights, take out knitting,

my russet room is warm, solitude lengthens, soothes
even while I wait for your call, your news.

Will You Come

Will you come when the day is ended
curtains drawn, fires lighted
tea ready on the range
smells of wood burning?

Will you come when the week is over
work done, put away for a day
grass mown, beds prepared
potatoes planted?

Will you come at the end of winter
rain easing, sun on the hills
even into evening, spring cleaning
primroses, daffodils?

Two Women

I've married two women, the first on fire,
her red field crying battle as
her nipples pierce mine like lances
and she defeats me without a tear.

My other wife is a good woman,
severe, distinguished, dark eyes alight;
her gentle breasts welcome me in
and I lie on her moss covered field,
come away eager to live.

Sometimes I leave the house of our marriage,
go down to the river, throw out my line,
hypnotised by clear water, mirages,
but when the hooked trout surfaces
fixing me with her frozen eyes

I run homeward, close the shutters,
burn myself on the pyre of my red wife,
cool down in the lake of my dark wife
for such is the sauna of my married life.

(Version of the poem, *Io ho sposato due Signore* by
    Euri Predonzani)

Against the Tide

My school rug

came with me across the water when they
waved goodbye on Dublin's North Wall.
There was no talk of comfort blankets then
but my rug served me well.

Before we bought our buttercup duck-down duvet,
fumbled it into a russet cover, we folded
my young rug around our shoulders,
lay together on a burnt umber pull-out sofa,
skin on skin tickled by tasselled fringes.

No longer soft as a sheep before shearing,
more hairy like an old goat in mountain passes,
the rug lies on the back seat of my car
ready for picnics or wrapping grandchildren
warm as they huddle after swims in Greystones.

I warn them not to pull hard at worn material
and when I shake out crumbs, damp sand,
light patches torn fabric,
green and brown checks.

My Woman
For my sister

My woman is a gardener,
grows seeds in her potting shed,
sweet peas, spinach, broad beans,
that she plants in a bed
dug over with humus,
good humour.

My woman's veined hand
kneads loaves of bread,
cuts fat into pastry,
weaves words into poetry,
makes patterns,
works them into shape.

My woman is old
wild and wise
has pearls in her eyes
tells stories in bed
long after lights out time.

Sylvan Theatre at Kilruddery

Zeus and Hera at home in bay hedges
welcome the audience to their theatre
a backdrop of trees, the sky a ceiling
watchers ranged on grass tiers.

At the centre the ravishing
of Persephone is carved on a stone throne,
three centuries of weather leave Hades headless.

Someone has moulded children's masks
on three boulders - their blank eyes,
their silent chorus.

Wind whips through hedges, clouds thicken,
the play is about to begin. Lear summons
his daughters, spectators long to warn him,
listen to your fool, learn who to trust
you're old enough to be wiser.

He won't take note of the cerulean sky
circling Cordelia's curls, prefers the murky
puffs of cloud shadowing his other girls.

No one can change the chronology

      blindness
             madness
                        mayhem

the audience applauds, actors bow.

Stars cluster and shine, the moon climbs high
lighting the gods left alone to their drama.
Zeus hangs his wife upside down in the sky
gold bracelets binding her wrists
iron anvils clasping her ankles.

Sacraments
For Mamo

When we visit you in hospital
your spirit will not dwell
on surgery, infection, instead

you show us the photograph
of a granddaughter in her
First Communion dress,

tell us the story of
your selection of special
samples of Clones lace

your research and designs,
every piece in place,
a handkerchief square
crowning long dark hair.

You took us to the
lace museum you helped set up
during hard times in Clones

but now we are wearing
white plastic disposable aprons
beside your ward bed

where only days earlier
your eleven children
with their families

were summoned,
where you received
the Last Rites.

Upper Lake, Glendalough

A notice warns us not to take the kids.
They're not abandoned, females graze nearby.
Disguised by trees and bracken, white tails
and beards shake the hillside stillness.

Four stand beside the lake, a longhaired male
waves curly horns at the nanny guarding
two piebald kids. They cross our path joining
eight others, giving no mind to photographers.

We walk by the water, gaze at Kevin's bed
discourse on holiness, why he is canonised,
a saint who pushed Kathleen into the lake
because she dared to love a holy man

and what made evangelists decide
sheep may be gathered in, goats cast aside.

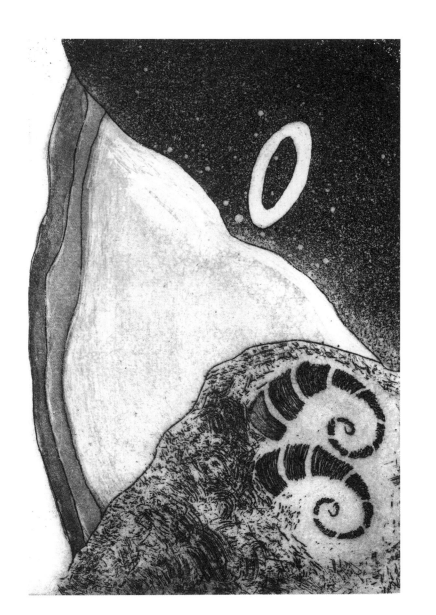

Tree of Life

Roots burrow underground
snake through anthracite
as branches complete the circle
interweaving, waving a lace mat
over the moon's citric face.

Did men converge on this grove
ages ago, set the fire, blow it alight
with iron bellows, performing rituals
around liturgical offerings?

I close my eyes, lean against the trunk
feel your spirit seep into my spine
envisaging their ceremonials
on one evening of revenge.

Priests are swaying in a ring
praying, not seeing one old woman
steal out of the undergrowth
to throw a lighted willow stick
into their dance.

Robes smoke, catch light, fireballs
crackle round the circle burning fingers
before they can sharpen knives.

Moaning they roll in damp leaves,
crawl away while women release virgins
cut through ropes that bit into their skin
rub on ointments, wrap them in linen gowns.

Now they're dancing to rhythms
of wind blowing through interstices
of branches, celebrating survival
in the sheltering forest.

A blackbird sings, I realise it's dawn
rub eyes, stretch out cramped legs
brush dry leaves from grass-stained jeans
and, wishing you good morning,
take my leave.

Vertigo

Three men and a woman
stretch over the edge
challenge each other
to hang out further,
young laughter.

Gulls,
their home on the cliff face,
perch in layers,
dive from crevices -
scream.

I move up the path
where cliffs are higher
the walkway narrows
and fewer people pass.

Now I'm on my own
watching waves break,
counting striations,
wavering reflections,

wind pushing my back
one long step down.

Leaving Inniskeen
For Patrick Kavanagh

The half-way house where cousins let us stay
has eased the journey from familiar land

near enough to look back on, as though
I'd never made the choice to go away,

leave stooks of reeds and ridged potato beds,
a cabbage patch with comfrey, fields

where the black and white of Friesians gather
for herding into milking sheds.

It was your garden roses and hollyhocks
I dreamed of when I drifted off to sleep

in a room smelling of polish, turf smoke,
boots that trudged through stones and muck

on the lane from family haggard to half-way house.
You offered to be with me on the way

for just the one night. In the morning
you'll take the road home. I will follow my muse.

What streets do I walk in this strange city
drinking with posers and poets in pubs without pity.

I'm always looking over my shoulder
at four green fields.

Against the Tide

They rowed their currach out of Renvyle Harbour
seven oarswomen moving with the rhythm
to Inishboffin, Grainuaile's island.

The hull was formed of timber frame with skins
stretched and tarred to hold against the tide
tested over sixty years of fishing.

Watchers of these women's shoreline meeting
never dreamt they planned a moonlit flit
thought they gathered for the evening's gossip

didn't know that under coloured shawls
they carried bread, pickled herrings
new potatoes, buttermilk they'd churned.

Surprised to see them push the dark craft out
and jump aboard, men shouted to each other
summoned sons and husbands, pointed at

the tough old boat that bore away their women,
grannies who were needed at the fireside
to mind the babies, help out with the cooking.

They cried, *the old ones must have lost their senses,*
didn't hear them singing as they rowed
a chorus wafting while the waves grew higher
hope still rising in old women's hearts.

Belfast Central

An hour to wait
for a train to Coleraine
time to explore as far
as the Waterfront Hall,

a display of photographs,
Burren limestone pavements
all grikes and wild flowers,
digital image of a kneeling girl

and here is the Giants Causeway,
Rathlin Island, Scotland within
arms reach on the horizon,
northern lights.

Lifted up to the second floor
I'm blown away by the panorama
of Belfast on water, Harland
and Wolff yellow cranes,

turn around, on the wall
a life size portrait, the poet
Michael Longley, in an aran cardigan,
earth-colours, looks over his glasses.

His study is scattered with plants,
shells, a dolphin's skull and poems.
Old friend, he welcomes me,
a stranger to his city.

Play On

Play On

We learned that music soothed the embryo
so your first tunes resounded in my womb
Hush little baby, don't say a word . . .

Water music played when you were born
face upwards, looking out into the world;
we heard *the pitter patter of the rain . . .*

You sang street songs all the way to school
to entertain your sister in her pram
I'll tell my Ma when I get home . . .

Heavy metal thrummed through every floor
until you turned to Gabriel, Marley, Ella
Summertime and the living is easy . . .

You and your girlfriend flew to Senegal,
learned new rhythms from a group of drummers -
on her continent you exchanged rings.

Home again, you chose your wedding hymns
changing words for ones you could believe in
Be thou my vision by day and by night,

You share your tales of tricky beasts and birds,
take turns or sing together to your baby
counting hours and breaths until the birth.

Photograph

taken before I was born
my father looks forward.
He foresaw the war,
signed up with the Sappers
in nineteen-thirty-nine
but died the April before.

I was nine months old,
so many things they never told us,
he was a silence in our lives.

Sweethearts in Manchester,
my mother an Irish Catholic
Daddy's profile Jewish.
Gran blessed their union.

You have a look of your father,
my friend tells me,
wish I'd grown up with him
I lift the photo from its frame
discover mother's printed words,

THE BEST OF THE BUNCH.

Old Long Hill

We were alone listening to wind in gorse
and water falling. Before we knew it
we had started the long trek up the hill
pacing on sleepers laid over boggy ground.

I never thought to reach the summit but you
were determined. I pressed on with pauses
to look down at waves riffling the lakeshore.
We met at the cairn where wind iced our faces.

I watched you bound downhill full tilt
while I minded my way, delighted with
the sight of white movement, a rump, others
grazing, ears pricked at our foot fall in grass.

This evening as I drive home from Glencree,
the moon rising over mountains, my headlights
catch the eye of one deer, the form of another
and I sense your footsteps on the road.

Birthday Present

After my long labour you were born
purple, they took you from me
put you in an incubator and we
could only look into that box
not hold or comfort you
as you struggled with light and air.

Years later in a hospital bed
we held you close, rubbed lavender oil
on your ankles, elbows, temples,
needles bruised violets on your skin
roses spread around your traction pins
rhododendron petals floated over burns.

Recovering, rucksack on your back,
you reach the land of the long white cloud,
swim with dolphins in ultramarine
twisting and curving in time with their spirits
bathe in hot streams under starlight
laughing with friends and old geysers.

I take your Maori jade from round my neck
trace its figure of eight, lick green flecked
stone, hold it to the light, this gift
you've sent across the world to me,
cushion it on purple and remember
all your ways of growing strong again.

Five year old poet

One swimmer skims through water
    falls under, surfaces, blows bubbles
        a pudgy hand splashes, reaches
            his laughing brother who

composes his poem, 'bum bump, bum bump,
    bum bump, not rhyme, the words
        don't have the same ending,
            it's alliteration.'

I lift my grandsons up, brown seals,
    wet flippers round my neck,
        feet flapping, beach them
            side by side on mummy's bed,

play our bedtime game wrapping them up
    in Nemo towels with fish, anemones,
        address the parcels to their Aunty Mary
            across the water as far as Enniskerry.

Space traveller he imagines their arrival,
    dogs sniff and lick, cousins come and play.
        'Tomorrow, Granny, you'll send us in a rocket
to Saturn and Jupiter, my favourite planets.'

a thrush sings look-out

you arrive with your African wife
and three little boys who transform

my home, slot lions and zebras
into the wooden train, play star wars

name stars, Orion's belt, Capricorn
the great bear in a mountain sky

a flying visit, sun reddens Dublin Bay
the morning you leave, we wave good bye

a single magpie steps onto the white line
striping a tarmac road.

Mountaineer

He dances
     his shadow on mine
runs ahead
     to catch his mother's
he wants to go
     all the way over rocks
again and again
     three years old
his first mountain climb.

Since he left us
     the sea is colder
stones are sharper
     boulders darker
shapes are shifting
     gate creaks gravel
wild strawberries all gone
     sheep and cows move on
the cot is folded away.

Harry

We've come to the churchyard,
planted flowers on your grave,
now make our way to Orford Quay

where every day, even when gales
blew off the North Sea,
you used to journey

bent almost at right angles to your stick,
stiff, aching, shrapnel still in your back
you'd sink onto a bench

with Mick, your companion,
beside you on a loose leash,
too old to pull the way he once did.

In this shelter facing Havergate,
island of green and red shanks, avocets,
knots, dunlins, terns, godwits,

we discover your form,
hold you there.

The Colditz Story

You never talked of Colditz before
but watching television you were cross
not because it stirred your memory of
four years interned, friends who died
from malnutrition, confinement
of fine minds

no, what got you was po-faced
officers plotting great escapes.
All that kept you and your mates
from going mad were laughs you had
the bloody funny tricks
which prisoners played.

I remember well that evening
when still in overalls muddied from
the haggard you held forth, back bent
with farm work, shrapnel caught at Crete
lodged on your spine, a spiteful sitting tenant.

After your stroke,
stuck in the wheelchair back to a Colditz
weight of seven stone, the words spit out
it hurts like hell, prisoner,
you fight your war again.

Artist's Print, Autumn Afternoon

Thirty years ago we looked together
      I said I'd been there too
could see myself in the hunch of your
      right shoulder. You gave me
           the etching.

You are the woman in the picture
      high cheekbones, short hair
one eyebrow arched, dark eyes
      ask questions
artist's mouth looks askance, your chin
      leads forward.

You hold your head in the left hand
      drawn larger than life
your right thumb holds an olive green
      mug of coffee
on the yellow wall behind, a charcoal
      drawing of hard blown trees.

Mother's Prayers

She fuels the kitchen range to boil water,
tips it on clothes in a deep stone basin,
rubs them with sunlight soap on a glass board,
calls us to mangle, hang washing on the line.

This is always on mondays when for tea
there's soup and sunday leftovers,
other days were fish or shepherds' pie
with semolina, junket, rice pudding.

In the evenings, she plays the piano
singing Shakespeare's dream songs
and Moore's melodies for Gran who loves
familiar lyrics, Mum's versions.

When we move to the farm in Tomhaggard
we bring in Friesian cows together
name them Daisy, Cowslip, Ragwort
in the dairy we separate milk, churn butter.

At the head of the oak table she settles
her will, framed oil painting of two girls
with long necks is my sister's, stooks
in a wild landscape are my pearls.

She contemplates children, grandchildren,
wondering who will inherit her night prayers
which last for ever. We tell her
she can take those with her to heaven.

Leaving

I was a child learning my mother,
her graceful figure, brown hair swept up,
slim ankles under a calf-length skirt.

We ran from school up to a blue front door,
blue like her eyes. 'Mummy, we're home.'
She'd hurry down the hall
hug us as we came in.

Today she struggles with doorknobs,
knotted knuckles, veined hands,
tries to smile and remember
the name she gave to her third child.
I put on her kettle, wash up mugs,
pour milk into a blue jug.

She no longer knows the time of day or seasons.
Have I had lunch yet? Tell me what you ate.
Every visit is a little more muddled,
certainties, faith in her prayers
failing like leaves left over to winter.

I cannot hear her songs.
When I was young
our house was filled with singing.
Books no longer please her
though she tries to read,
to write us letters.

I put my coat on,
don't leave me now,
she whispers.

Mary Breen

And then there was dear Breenie in the kitchen
always making room there for us children
when we ran in from school,

laid our homework on the table.
Once done, we'd clear it off and help her
get the tea with treats like dripping toast,

potato cakes or fresh baked scones with butter,
plum jam, honey. She'd always be there
except on Fridays when she went to church

and prayed for us but much more for her son
who'd gone to London, taken to drink and died there,
when he was only twenty-one.

She rarely talked of him but one night
my brother stumbled in, a few drinks taken
and she tore into him.

A Slaney woman, she used to buy the Wexford
Free Press every week; we'd tease her,
call it the Wexford Liar, how could she call it free

when money changed hands? We thought
she'd be pleased when my stepfather
bought a farm near Tomhaggard,

in the Barony of Forth and Bargay,
we children had left home by then,
but she demurred, didn't want

this closeness to her kin as none had spoken
to her since her son was born. In the end
she moved down. Her country ways

informed the work of handling broody hens,
churning butter, bringing the cows in,
her chair beside the Aga

the heart of the home.

Swan

For Conor (1956 – 1996)

On Friday you died at home,
children snuggled close,
measuring breaths.

Your email said
I'm climbing Sugarloaf.
Now you've reached the summit

can you see us in a churchyard
at the mountain's foot, chucking
earth and tears onto your coffin?

The river laps onto a muddy beach
where one swan buries her beak
under a cushioned wing.

we take our leave
i.m. Andrew

your evening laughter
will never be heard
in the long twilight
of an April birthday

like a dream
you are present here
and stay with us
in our present loss

time inches away
forwards again
you are a child playing
you are the best of men

cold rain spills
on a waiting grave
your brothers lower the coffin
on dark red ribbons

your baby son smiles
in the arms of your lover
your father and mother
throw petals.

Visit

One year after her funeral,
three from his, my brother
and I visit their grave.

First we call at the Walled Garden,
search out shrubs hardy enough
for Orford Churchyard

then carry, as offerings to ancestors,
white-flowered hebe, violet pansies,
borrow a trowel from neighbours,

plant, heel and water them in.
Beside the sandstone we say a prayer
that they're getting along.

Geraniums

To-day, first Sunday free of frost
after this longest winter, I carry out
my red geranium, take cuttings
and plant them in pots of compost
as presents for our sons as they leave

and remember Gran filling
the conservatory with mauve, purple
and white scented flowers

feeding them tea leaves,
coffee grounds
and dregs of chamber pots,
coaxing with verses of her poets,

Milton, Shakespeare, Wordsworth.

When our daughter went exploring
from Amazon Rain Forest
to Anapurna Range she left me

her green plants with one geranium
saying, talk to them,
so I tell my poems
read her letters aloud.